EARLY DAYS

Swinton's very early history may well be associated with the Northern Britons of the Brigantes tribe. The Brigantes held an impressive hill fort at Wincobank and Swinton's lands most likely came under their lordship.

At times during the Roman invasion, the legions had to overcome violent resistance from the Brigantes who would have used natural defences such as rivers in their battle plans. As Swinton is sited on higher ground to the River Don, we can speculate that the area witnessed some desperate hand to hand combat.

Evidence of Roman presence has been verified. In 1853, workers digging out a cellar on Rockingham Road uncovered a hoard of 300-400 coins covering the period from 69 to 212 AD. We have no idea who the hoarder was nor what became of him. Further indication of Roman activity is the existence of two roads crossing the area which would have linked the Templeborough Roman fort near Rotherham with territory to the North.

The Romans withdrew back to their capital in around 410. Western Europe then entered the Dark Ages. It is believed, however, that Swinton's impressive ancient earthwork, the Rig Dyke, was constructed during this period. For many years it was believed that the Dyke dated from the Roman period and it was named the 'Roman Rig'. More recent theories have suggested that the earthworks may well have been a boundary between Anglo-Saxon Kingdoms of Northumbria and Mercia. The Kingdom of Elmet to the North may also have played a part. The truth of our Rig Dyke's origins is shrouded in the mists of time, but we can be sure that Swinton was a borderland.

During the centuries of the Dark Ages, Barbarian tribes such as the Angles and Saxons invaded and settled much of England. The River Don would have provided a watery highway to assist this migration.

Norman Conquest

As we know from our school days, William the Conqueror's Norman invasion took place in 1066. William defeated the Saxon King Harold's forces at Hastings after Harold had forced marched his army from Stamford Bridge, Near York.

The Norman's began their ascendancy and England was parcelled out to William's followers as a reward for their services. The Doomsday Book, completed in 1086, was an audit of the property and resources available to England's new masters.

At the time of the Doomsday Survey, Swinton was very sparsely inhabited and was an area of mostly waste and wood pasture. We do, however, get an agreement over the place name of Swinton deriving from the old English for "Swine Farm". Documents in Latin dating from very ancient times refer to the settlement as Villa Porcorum (House of Pigs).

Places of Worship

The Norman chapel of St. Mary Magdalene was built in the second half of the 12th century, as a chapel of ease for the Parish of Wath. It stood on the site of the present St. Margaret's Church Hall and, at one time, had the town's cross nearby and a set of stocks. Interestingly, Chapel Hill was the site of the town's first pub. The chapel may have been the work of the famous Knights of St. John of Jerusalem who had lands and buildings in Swinton.

The chapel was sadly demolished in 1816.

Close by was the Old Hall, believed to be the residence of King John's principal butler. King John (1199 -1216) would have been a house guest when he journeyed in this part of his realm.

The Parish Church of St. Margaret was consecrated on June 15, 1817, the patron being the then Earl Fitzwilliam who gave the land. It wasn't until 1851 that Swinton became a separate parish, independent of Wath and Mexborough.

On March 24th, 1897, a catastrophic fire burnt down the original church, with only the tower surviving. The present larger church was built on to the old tower and was consecrated on October 28th, 1899.

The clock in the church tower was installed in 1937 to celebrate the Coronation of King George VI.

The rapid industrialisation of the Victorian period lead to extensive housing development and other building in the Swinton Bridge area of the town. To serve this community, St. Michael's Church was constructed on White Lea Road as a chapel of ease to the main Church. St. Michael's opened on August 15th, 1901. It is now demolished and no trace remains on the site.

Swinton's population in 1800 was 653, which by 1901 had exploded to 12,217.

This rapid increase in population corresponded with the building of other churches and chapels. St. John's Methodist Church was rebuilt in 1910 replacing an original Wesleyan Chapel dating from 1865. A Congregational School was erected in Station Street in 1884, and a Congregational Church was opened on the site in 1902.

A Wesleyan Reform Chapel, The Ebenezer Church, was opened on Milton Street in 1873. This building was demolished in 2000. In 1869, a Methodist Chapel opened on Bridge Street, being demolished about a century later. Today, other places of Christian Worship occupying later buildings can be found with the Bethany Church, Rowms Lane, Bow Broom Chapel, Queen Street, Zion Gospel Church, Charles Street and the Piccadilly Methodist Church on Piccadilly Road.

THE PLAGUE

In June 1646 Swinton was visited by the Plague which raged in the town until October of that year. Some 59 persons were recorded as victims, at that time this represented a third of the population.

During the construction work on Swinton Church Hall in 1913, a mass grave of human remains was uncovered, believed to be plague victims. The remains were re-interred in Swinton churchyard which, at 9 acres, in size is one of the largest open churchyards in the country.

WORLD FAMOUS POTTERIES

Edward Butler first established his tile and pot works in Swinton in 1745. The site off Blackamoor Road was ideal for a pottery with clay available on Swinton Common, a reliable water supply, building stone quarried from Wath Wood and coal obtainable from close by.

Eventually, control passed into the hands of the Brameld family, whose technical competence enabled the pottery to become world famous, with an international sales base and royal clients. Rising costs caused the factory to close in 1842.

A further world-famous Swinton Pottery was the Don Pottery at the other end of town, nearby Kilnhurst had the Twigg Pottery. Products from these potteries are now highly sought after in the antiques world with collectors of ceramics world-wide maintaining a keen interest in Swinton's pots.

SCHOOLS

An early record of educational provision was a school provided by the Earl Fitzwilliam for his stable lads who worked at Swinton Racecourse (the racecourse was, in the main, a training grounds which did produce one Lincoln winner between the wars.). A Church School opened on Church Street in 1854, with enlargements in 1900 and 1910. This became known as the Fitzwilliam County School. The buildings remain today as private residences. The Education Board erected a school at Swinton Bridge in 1878 and at Queen Street in 1908. Queen Street School still serves the children of the town, along with Fitzwilliam Infants, Fitzwilliam Juniors and Brookfield Junior and Infant Schools. Secondary education, including VI form, is provided by Swinton Community School, which started life in 1958 as a teacher-training establishment.

COAL

Coal has been worked in the Swinton area certainly since 1600. Early mining was by the use of bell pits, opencast and drift methods. The deep mined Manvers Colliery opened in 1870 and Wath Main in 1875 heralded the era of the super pits and population growth in the area necessitated corresponding urban expansion.

OTHER INDUSTRIES AND TRANSPORT

Waterways have played an important part in Swinton's past as the town was an important junction of the Dearne and Dove Canal and the Sheffield & South Yorkshire Navigation. Boat building in the town started in 1770 and the tradition was carried on later by Thomas Scholey and the Waddington family.

Railways first came with the North Midland line and the first station opened in 1840 at the site of our present interchange. A new station was built by the Midland Railway slightly to the north of this. This opened in 1899 and closed in 1968. The Manchester, Sheffield and Lincolnshire Railway came through Swinton around 1870 and Swinton Central Station opened. The present Swinton Interchange opened in 1990, restoring rail services to the town after a gap of 22 years. In 2002, the facility was presented with a National Award for the best Small Interchange in the U.K.

On the production side, Burnett's Wagon Works produced rail vehicles and wheels from their premises on White Lea Road.

The Iron and Steel industry was well represented by Baker & Bessemer at Kilnhurst. These works turned out a whole range of products, including railway and tram wheels and munitions. Brothers Thomas and Charles Hattersley moved to Swinton from Sheffield in 1864. They went on to establish a large and prosperous industrial enterprise on Whitelea Road called Queens Foundry. A wide range of products were made, including many types of domestic and industrial heating equipment and home appliances. The works had a strong record of entering their products in trade and industrial fairs. The heating industry is still manufacturing in Swinton at the Stelrad Plant.

Swinton was home to the glass industry from the 1850's until 1988 trading under a number of names, e.g. Dale & Browns and United Glass Containers.

At the end of World War II, the General Electric Company took over a former munitions factory at the side of the River Don. Cookers were produced in prodigious numbers as the factory grew into one of the largest cooker plants in the Empire. Morphy Richards Limited now manages the plant which continues to employ significant numbers of local people.

Swinton's many other industries, both past and present have included chemicals, mineral waters, plastic products, foodstuffs, vehicles and much more!

THE WORLD WARS

As with most communities, Swinton suffered grievous losses of young men in World War I. 207 names are recorded on our fine War Memorial, including that of Tommy Jackson, V.C. Tommy was the first British soldier to cross the mighty Hindenburg Line in 1918. On the home front, Zeppelins dropped a number of bombs in the Swinton area which, fortunately, only broke some windows.

During World War II, the casualty list was, thankfully, much lighter but still spelt tragedy for the families involved. Swinton's first resident to be killed in Action was my family cousin, Sidney Bell, who died at sea off the coast of Norway. The last death was William Philips, who died in 1946 in Montagu Hospital.

We must not forget the vital contribution of those of our residents who kept vital industries and services working. In addition, many contributed to the war effort in the Home Guard, etc. The tower of Swinton Church was used by fire watchers who would have spent many a cold night out after a day at work.

Very large sums of money were raised by the Local War Savings Association. Their efforts were so successful, in fact, that the entire cost of a trawler minesweeper was raised in 1942. This was adopted as Swinton's ship and was named "HMS Kingston Jacinth". Unfortunately the vessel was sunk by a mine with the loss of several of her crew.

This book seeks to present a pictorial history of the town by the use of pictures and captions.

Many of the photographs we have used have not been seen in the public domain previously, other shots will be familiar to some people. We consider some of these as classic images and well worthy of bringing to the attention to new audiences.

The book is divided into four broad chapters or themes.

Firstly we look at <u>People,</u> the most precious component of any community.

Then we consider Swinton as a <u>Place</u>, and see how some things have changed very little over the years while other sites are almost unrecognisable.

Thirdly we examine <u>Transport</u>. Swinton has been a very important place regarding various types of transport over the years. There is of course a very important railway junction in the town and this has ensured that a good range of destinations can be reached by rail from our attractive Transport Interchange. In earlier times an equally important canal junction led to the development of the town as a waterways centre.

Turnpike highways passed through and these have now been absorbed into the road network. Our transport chapter includes railways, canals, tramways, trolley-buses, motor-buses and other road vehicles.

Finally we look at aspects of <u>Work</u>. This study includes prime, heavy, light and creative industry. We also take at look at public services and business life.

The authors hope that you enjoy "Old Swinton" (in pictures).

We are always on the look-out for other photographs, memorabilia, ephemera etc. which could be used in future projects and be added to the archive.

Please get in touch if you have any material that you would be glad to share.

Ken Wyatt and Giles H. Brearley September 2005

ACKNOWLEDGEMENTS AND PICTURE CREDITS

Giles Brearley and Ken Wyatt would like to thank the following people for their help and assistance in the completion of this project.

Jean and Phillip Thornton, Dorothy Stone, Mrs Wilkinson, Brian Hobson, Alan Downing, the family of Clara and William Badger, Ron James, the Warren Family, Andrew Liversidge, Mike Trowbridge, Barry Wright, Ivan Randerson, Alan Peace, John Howitt, Nancy Whaley, John and Mike McNamara, Brearley and Co. Accountants, Mrs. H. Ward, Neil Lawrence, John Clayton, Mexborough and Swinton Trolley Bus Group, Swinton Bridge Action Group, Molly Buckley, Rotherham Metropolitan Borough Council, South Yorkshire Times, Dearne Valley Weekender, Star Newspapers, The Laird of Camster, Alan Hobson, Barry Lowkes, Tony Greenfield, the Butterfield family, Richard Drakeford.

Our apologies for any omission, no offence is intended, so many people have offered advice, information and encouragement, We are grateful to everyone.

PEOPLE

Mrs. Priscilla Drakeford (nee White). Mrs. Drakeford was the wife of Ernest Dixon Drakeford, who was a survivor of the torpedoing of the RMS Lusitania. Both Ernest and "Cilla" kept a confectioners shop on Bridge Street, Swinton, near to the old Bridge Street Methodist Church of which they were both active members. After Ernest died, Mrs. Drakeford continued to run the shop alone until it closed around 1968. In this photograph, she is a very attractive young lady – in later years her hair was pure white. Priscilla died 13 November, 1975, aged 90. The full story of Ernest's experiences can be read in "The Lusitanian's Musician" by Ken Wyatt, ISBN 1-904706-05-03.

A celebration of 'Empire Day' taken in the early years of the C20th. The procession of children heads down Station Street towards the Bridge Area. The row of cottages was located along Station Street opposite to the Masonic Hall. These were very small mainly privately rented dwellings. Even up to their final clearance in the 1960s, these cottages had only a cold water supply, outside toilets, and no fitted baths. The row of steps up to the front of the cottages was located near to where Highcliffe Drive begins.

Residents pictured outside the pub known as the "Goose with Two Necks" have gone to a great deal of trouble decorating the building and street to celebrate the Jubilee of Queen Victoria. Note the large amount of horse droppings in the road. Through most of these buildings are gone this part of Fitzwilliam Street is still recognisable looking down the 'one way' section towards Milton Street.

Hamshaw Bridge on 21st May 1905. A large crowd of people are moving up from the Mexborough end of the town as they participate in the Swinton Convalescent Home Sunday procession. A body of 8 policemen march in front of the parade followed by a military unit wearing their medals. A contemporary report states that some £4 4s 4d was gathered in the collection boxes. Three pubs can be identified, The Canal Tavern, Red House and Ship Inn. The houses on the right of the picture stand on what is now Broomville Gardens. The prominent sign advertises Thomas Scholey's Boatyard.

Councillor John Bingham, Chairman of Swinton UDC in 1910. The Council was established in 1894 and Councillor Bingham was the 12th person to be Chairman. He was the licensee of the canal tavern in addition to his public duties.

3

Alfred and Emily Liversidge, residents of Charles Street and later, Middleton Villas, Fitzwilliam Street. Alf was in his younger days Britain's fastest man, a runner in many road races. He went on to become a very successful boxing trainer, training the United Kingdom's last bare knuckle Heavyweight champ Jem Mace.
Alfred and Emily had seven children. Alfred died 21ˢᵗ January 1921.

A photograph of Alfred Liversidge Junior. This young man was deaf, he was also noted to have great skills dealing with horses.

4

Alfred Augustus Wilson, one of the 207 sons of Swinton to lose his life in WW1 with his sister Lavinia. The family resemblance is quite striking.

A close up of Alfred Wilson he was killed in action 27th April 1918 while his battalion was in trenches next to Le Grand Bois on the outskirts of Wytschaete in Flanders. Alfred lived at 261 Queen Street he was the son of Harriet Harvey (formerly Wilson) and the late Albert Wilson a native of Mexborough. Alfred is buried in Wytshaete Military Cemetery and was 29 years old when he was killed.

1912 and the royal party of King George V motors from Wentworth Woodhouse to Cadeby Colliery. Here the convoy passes by the Carnegie Library cheered on by enthusiastic spectators. The King was visiting Cadeby soon after two terrible explosions had occurred. The first blast killed 35 men, a further 53 died in the second explosion.

A group of boy pupils at Swinton Bridge School taken in the 1920's. Some of the boys are quite smartly dressed, while others show signs of poverty – most manage a cheeky grin for the camera. At this time the sexes were strictly segregated in the school environment only getting to mix on very special occasions. Boys and Girls had separate entrances to school and different play areas.

A huge crowd at the dedication of Swinton's War Memorial in 1921. The ceremony was attended by the Earl Fitzwilliam who had donated the land. Built in the style of "The Cross of Sacrifice" designed by architect Sir Reginald Bloomfield, the memorial commemorates 207 Swinton residents who were victims of WW1. After WW2, a further plaque was added with the names of 41 casualties inscribed on it.

A close up of the platform party including various clergy, military representatives, V.I.P.s and the Earl Fitzwilliam at the war memorial dedication.

A group of Senior Scouts and Leaders at their annual camp in around 1936, the event involved many Swintonians. A home movie film of the event can be seen on the History of Swinton Vol. 3 video produced by Swinton Heritage.

Swinton's Auxiliary Fire Service in 1940 outside of their headquarters to the rear of Highfield House. These firemen formed part of Swinton Civil protection and air raid precautions services which during WW2 were under the control of Mr Basil Bower the Town Clerk. An emergency H.Q. was located in the cellars of the Carnegie Library. Swinton's Auxiliary Fire Service was called upon to help after the Sheffield Blitz in December 1940. Fortunately Swinton was spared enemy action but did lose 41 sons and daughters as war dead.

Stanley Vicars, a WW2 casualty. Stanley was in the Navy serving on the aircraft carrier, HMS Glorious. The Glorious was lost along with 263 squadron of the Fleet Air Arm on 8th June 1940. She was sailing towards Scapa Flow escorted by a pair of destroyers when she was spotted by the powerful German battle-cruisers Scharnhorst and Gneisenau. The German ships opened fire at a range of 20,000 yards, gaining direct hits on the bridge of the carrier. Glorious returned fire with her own armament but was hopelessly out of range. Soon the carrier was dead in the water and sinking fast. The two destroyers, Ardent and Acasta, did their brave and suicidal best to protect their charge, but both were sunk. From the three British vessels 1,519 lost their lives, including 1,207 from the HMS Glorious, one of whom was Swinton resident Stan Vicars.

Harold Ward, Swinton born hero. Hal Ward was born in 1912 on William Street, and attended Swinton Bridge School. After leaving school, he began work as a coal miner. The start of his working life coincided with the terrible strike of 1926. After three years working as a miner, Hal decided to join the Royal Navy. During the Second World War, her served in the battle of the Atlantic, and in other theatres. At the end of the war, he remained in the Navy as a professional sailor. Mr Ward had

progressed through the non-commissioned ranks and was promoted to lieutenant. In 1955, whilst serving in the Mediterranean, his ship was called upon to assist an Italian oil tanker by the name of Argea Prima, which had caught fire. Lieutenant Ward led the boarding party from his ship to the tanker, where they assisted the Italian crew to abandon ship. Mr Ward then went on to carry out the very risky procedure of closing various hatches around the tanker to control the spread of the fire. Fire fighting operations then commenced, eventually the tanker was saved, and an environmental catastrophe was averted. Hal Ward was awarded the Queen's commendation for bravery by her Majesty Queen Elizabeth II.

These photographs show Cleggs Cottage No. 7 Wentworth Road which stood opposite the junction of Blackamoor Road and the B6090 Wentworth Road. The property dated originally from the 1600's and was also known as the Salt House.

The tenants of the cottage from the early 1920's till 1946 were William and Clara Badger shown hear stood in their yard [above right]. Mr Badger was a miner who during part of his working life worked at Warren House Colliery a short distance from his home. The cottage was rented from the Fitzwilliam Estate who also owned the colliery. During the second world war in December 1941 Sheffield was badly bombed. Two stray bombs fell near to Cleggs Cottage one on each side of the road. When help arrived the old couple were found covered in soot but otherwise unharmed. William joked that at least the Germans cleaned the chimney!

Mr and Mrs Badger amazingly had 13 children, 8 of whom are pictured below. All are now deceased but many of their grandchildren (and other descendants) live in the area. Cleggs' cottage was demolished in the immediate post war period as it was considered unsafe due to the effects of coal extraction.

A group of local residents pose on Highfield Road, Swinton. No T.V. aerials or satellite dishes are visible on the houses and the roadside trees have grown significantly since this photograph was taken.

Swinton Town band descend from Hamshaw Bridge. The Ship Inn can be seen in the background and rough ground occupies what is today Broomville Gardens which were landscaped in 1953. Cobble stones form the road surface which must have been very uncomfortable for cyclists.

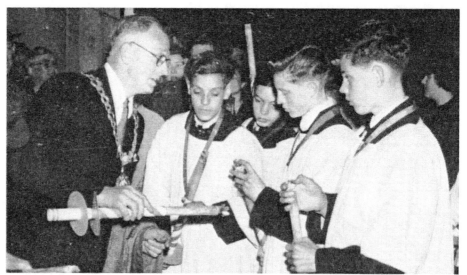

Councillor Ernest Edgar Shaw and members of St Margaret's Church choir light candles prior to a parade to mark the coronation of Queen Elizabeth II in 1953.

The 2ⁿᵈ Don and Dearne Swinton scout troop stand proudly before the celebratory arch which they built to commemorate the coronation of Queen Elizabeth in 1953. Swinton celebrated the coronation in considerable style with a full programme of events organised by a committee of local people.

1953 and members of Swinton Urban District Council march at the head of the procession that paraded through the town. Starting at Market Street, the parade went via Bridge Street, Station Street, Church Street, Rockingham Road, Broadway, Rookery Road and Park Road terminating on the Miners' Welfare Grounds. A grand gala was held on the field including dance displays by local children. In the evening, a bonfire and firework display lit up the skies above Highfield Park. In this photograph, Councillor Ernest Edgar Shaw, Chairman and Mrs. Shaw, Consort, lead the way. Councillor Bill Bentham is 3rd row back nearest the camera. The leading cart carries children representing Queen Bodiccea.

Group photograph of the 2nd Don and Dearne Swinton Scouts taken in St Margaret's Church Hall in 1953. Senior Scout Master was Eddie Trowbridge of Trowbridge and Trowbridge Builders. Eddie was very well respected and had been scout master for many years prior to this date.

St John's Road 1956 and a family group stand with their visitors outside of their brand new council house. Behind the group of people are open fields where later St Mary's Crescent was to be built by Ben Bailey Construction Ltd.

This photograph is of children of the Butterfield family and was taken at Wood Street. The youngsters are Ronald, Lillian and Mildred Butterfield children of C.T. Butterfield. The other children are Kenneth Butterfield, Donald Reed and Margaret Steel who were grandchildren.

Members of Mexborough Rotary Club participating in a tree planting ceremony on Rowms Lane in the early 1950s. These trees have now reached considerable maturity.

Local Artist Ervin Pugh paints a portrait of Edward (Ted) Dobson who was a local scrap metal merchant. Mr. Pugh was commissioned to paint this portrait in 1957. He lived on Rockingham Road, Ted lived at 23 Twyford Close his business premises were on Rowms Lane.

Councillor Mrs Lawrence is seen receiving a presentation from Mrs Beattie Horton on the right. Other ladies of the Swinton Labour Party Women's Section look on.

Signatures of the Swinton Labour Party Women's section involved in the presentation to Mrs Lawrence. We believe that all these ladies have now passed away.

Councillor Mrs Lawrence when she was Chair of S.U.D.C. This is the occasion of Mrs Lawrence opening a new control unit of the Swinton Sewage Works located at Swinton Meadows at the side of the River Don. For many years sanitation and water supply was a great problem for the Swinton district. There were frequent shortages of water and outbreaks of cholera and other water borne diseases. An efficient sewage disposal system is a crucial public health requirement and the opening of Swinton Sewage Works in the 1930's was a significant event.

A happy group of management and Union representatives in the Masonic Hall, Swinton, on the occasion of presentation of long service awards by Messrs. Hattersley Brothers.

Two young children blowing the "angels" of dandelions as they sit in Horsefair Park. Behind them can be seen the semi-detached houses of Manor Road. The local name for this public open space for many years was "Council Field". The area acquired this name because the horses that were used to pull the vehicles of Swinton UDC, like dust carts, were grazed on this field during their off duty time.

Frank Wright, with a young friend outside of his home at 6 St John's Road. Frank was a very well known figure in the district. In his younger days, he was a keen footballer, cricketer and tennis player, before developing severe rheumatoid arthritis. Frank worked at Baker and Bessemer. Frank was always known for his cheerfulness and positive outlook on life. He had a very sharp mind maintaining a keen interest in politics, sport and all manner of local affairs. Frank was born in Bolton-Upon-Dearne in 1916 and died at home on Christmas morning 1976.

Jack and Dorothy Trowbridge stand in front of their Ford Anglia on a trip to the moors. Jack, and his brother, Eddy, took over the building firm on the death of their father, Frederick George Trowbridge, in 1936. Frederick had been one of Swinton's oldest and most respected master builders. Originally, he was a native of Wilt-shire but had lived in the town from an early age. At one time, he worked with the firm "J. Bower" but afterwards became a partner in the firm of Smith & Trowbridge. George was always interested in stone, in his youth he worked in the quarries at Mexborough and Hooton Roberts. He was highly skilled in the art of building dry walls and an all round expert mason. Jack and Eddy had a brother Allan and a sister Mary. The family lived at "Stoneglen", 32 Church Street.

May 1996 saw a visit to Swinton by the 2 daughters of Harry Crossley former British Cruiserweight Boxing Champion and Swinton resident. They had come to unveil a plaque to Harry and his brother Herbert who was British Heavyweight Novice Champion. During their visit the ladies donated Harry's Championship Boxing Gloves to Swinton Heritage. The gloves can be viewed in Swinton Library, while the plaque is attached to the corner shop premises at the junction of Queen Street and Church Street.

A group of Swinton residents believed to be posing in the playground of Swinton Bridge School.

Form 21 Swinton Comprehensive School September 1970. Mr Lomas was the form teacher and the group included many 'characters'. Among the boys are pictured Duncan Marklew, Christopher Hague (Eggy), John Rajman (Rajji), Steven Sutton, David Batty, Charles Clinton (Charlie) and Steven Haythorn (Aggie). The girls include Dianne Vickers, Alison Batson, Lynn Axon and Diane Kemp.

Swinton Cyclist Mike McNamara receiving a cup one of his many awards. Mike began cycle racing in 1951. He went on to become 12 times North Midlands Best All-rounder and Yorkshire Best All-rounder 1965-68-74 & 77. He was British Best All-rounder in 1967 and led the Rockingham (Swinton) Cycling Club as team winners in 1974, 76, and 77. Mike became the British 12hr Champion in 1966 over 258.2 miles. He established the British 50 Miles record in 1964 at 1hr 51mins 49 seconds, and broke the British 12hr record in 1967 covering 276½ miles. In 1976 Mike was presented with the C.A. Rhodes memorial award for outstanding achievements in the realms of Yorkshire cycling.

Ernest Wild, champion angler of Swinton, shows off some of his impressive array of trophies and medals.

Senior Aircrafts Woman Jane Wyatt of Swinton meets Her Majesty Queen Elizabeth II on 12th March 1971 during a Royal Visit to RAF Brize Norton. Jane, a former pupil of Kilnhurst & Queen Street Junior School and Swinton Comprehensive joined the RAF aged 17 years. She went on to serve in Cyprus as part of the U.N. Forces.

Councillor Frank Calladine pulls the first pint (Heineken Lager) at the opening of Swinton Civic Hall in 1972. Mr. Calladine wears the Chairman of the Council's Chain of Office while Mrs. Calladine wears the smaller Consort's Chain. Both Chains have the Swinton badge as a pendant.

Basil Bower in bowler hat. This shot was taken in Weston-Super-Mare not long before the second world war whilst attending a local government conference. Mr Bower, a qualified solicitor served as Swinton's Town Clerk from 1919 till his death in 1948. During the war years he was controller of the Town's emergency and air raid precautions services. During the First World War he was a Captain in the York and Lancaster Regiment.

Members and officers of Swinton Urban District Council. They are back row left to right Bob O'Donahugh – Treasurer, Brian Hobson – Councillor, Cyril Batson – Engineer, Kenneth Alldred- Clerk to the Council, Roland Benton- Councillor, Donald Barnes- Deputy Clerk, Douglas Thompson- Councillor. Middle row, Albert Newsam- Councillor, Winnie Lawrence-Councillor, Ted Fuller- Public Health Inspector, Jack Haythorne- Councillor, Oscar Hartley- Councillor, Michael Eagleton- Councillor, Thirza Myers- Councillor, John Willy Taylor- Councillor, Jack Kerry – Housing Manager. Front row, Jack Beck – Councillor, George Reader – Councillor, Frank Calladine – Councillor Enoch Sykes –Councillor. After Swinton Urban District Council was abolished in 1974 and the area became part of the administrative district of Rotherham Metropolitan Borough Mesers Calladine, Thompson and Benton were elected to represent the Swinton Ward on that body. It is worth noting that some of the councillors are wearing a medal type of badge. This indicated that the individual was a past Chairman of the Council, the men are also wearing corporate council ties.

Councillor R. Benton of Swinton was Mayor of Rotherham in 1977/78. In this photograph "Rolly" is attending a presentation evening at Hattersley Brothers, a very nice looking carvery and salad is about to be enjoyed. The venue was the works' Social Club located at the Mexborough side of Queens Foundry.

Retirement presentation to Tom Walton on 26ᵗʰ September, 1985. Tom had served with the South Yorkshire Ambulance Service for 19 years. Before that he had been a police officer. Tom was, for much of his service, Branch Secretary of the Ambulance Branch of the National Union of Public Employees. He held senior National positions within that trade union and had worked on National negotiations with Rodney Bickerstaff. In this shot, Tom receives his retirement cheque from the NUPE Branch Chairman, Ken Wyatt.

The mainly Swinton and Kilnhurst based Dearne Valley CND group in London to participate in a demonstration about the deployment of US controlled Cruise Missiles on U.K. Soil. During the early 1980's the groups' membership was well over 100 people.

Peter Hardy (later Lord Hardy of Wath) Member of Parliament for Wentworth till 1997 which included the Swinton Ward. Peter on the left, is pictured here with the then Member of Parliament for Rotherham Stan Crowther. The M.P's were participating in a rally in Rotherham's All Saints Square 14th November 1983.

To commemorate the United Nations International Year of Peace the public garden at the junction of Rookery Road and Church Street was named Swinton Peace Garden. Here the Mayor of Rotherham Councillor Jack Skelton unveils the plaque as from the left looking on are Mrs Skelton (Mayoress) Jack Taylor, President of the Yorkshire area National Union of Mineworkers, Norman West, Member of the European Parliament for Yorkshire South and Jack Mulcahy one of the principal organisers of the event.

Following the unveiling a large parade, led by a majorette band, marched from Swinton to Mexborough Athletic Club.

Peace was the theme of the march and various banners were in evidence. Norman West, Jack Mulcahy and Jack Taylor here lend a hand with a banner on a rather wet autumnal morning.

Inside Swinton Library, 2000 at a ceremony to re-dedicate the war memorial which was recovered from the old Ebenezer Church, that stood on Milton Street. From the left Councillor John Doyle, Councillor Michael Eagleton J.P., Councillor Michael Judge – Mayor of Rotherham, Reverend Nigel Williamson – Vicar of Swinton and Tommy Gear of the Swinton & Kilnhurst Royal British Legion.

Chris Andrews, professional photographer and brother of Hollywood megastar Julie Andrews. Chris has visited Swinton on behalf of the family to view locations associated with his maternal grandfather, William Arthur Morris. Mr. Morris was resident in Swinton during the 1920's; he was known as the Pitman's Poet and performed in a club act with his musical daughter Barbara (Chris and Julie Andrew's mother). For the full story see "The Pitman's Poet "by Giles Brearley.

Eddie Trowbridge at 100 years of age, he had been living in the USA for some years.

In 2001 members of the Swinton Bridge Action Group created this rockery on a previously neglected site on Bridge Street. Materials such as top soil, tree bark, canal stone, plants and the supply of earth- moving equipment was donated by a number of local businesses. The plaque was supplied and fitted by C.T. Butterfields – all the labour was provided by local residents some of whom can be seen here after completing their hard work.

Members of Swinton Bridge Action Group "in action" on a Sunday morning community clean-up day – of the canal and bank-side adjacent to White Lee Road. Wading in the canal wearing a Yellow jacket is the late Barry Best who was a very valued member of the group.

On Sunday 12th September 2004 a service of re-dedication was held on Chapel Hill Green to commemorate the restoration and re-locating of Swinton Town Cross. The clergy who participated were from left to right; Rev. Joseph Kiaga, St John's Methodist Church; Father Christopher Barley, Vicar of Swinton; The Venerable Robert Fitzharris, the Arch-Deacon of Doncaster; and Rev. Nigel Elliot, Vicar of Kilnhurst.

15th January 2005 and people gather at the Junction of Rowms Lane and Marriott Road to witness the unveiling of a commemorative plaque to a well loved former Swinton resident Tony Capstick.

Tony spent his childhood years living on White Lee Road, Swinton, attending the nearby Swinton Bridge School, which he always remembered with affection. Tony was a multi-talented individual who was well known in the folk music circuit, as an actor, song writer and broadcaster. He had a hit record "Capstick comes home," appearing on Top of the Pops. His T.V. work included 'Last of the Summer Wine'. For many years Tony was a Radio Sheffield presenter who cultivated many friendships among his huge following of listeners.

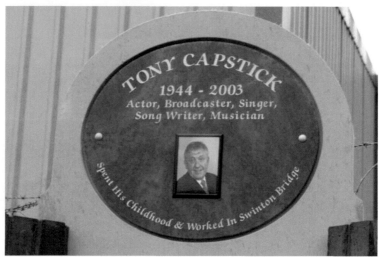

His widow Jill unveiled this plaque which proudly stands opposite his old school.

PLACE

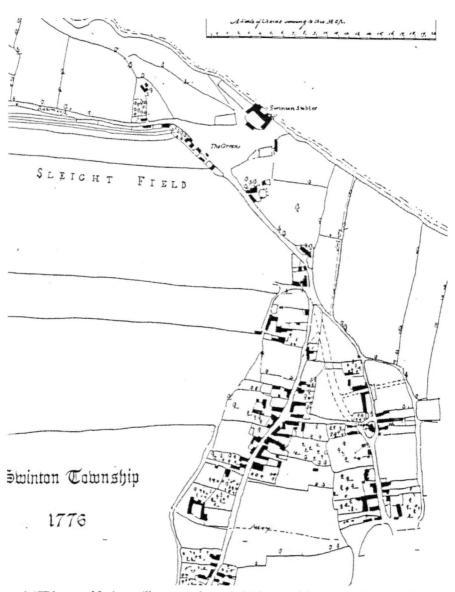

A 1776 map of Swinton illustrates the main highway of the town to be Fitzwilliam Street. Swinton Stables are shown towards the top but most of the built environment is clustered around Fitzwilliam Street. The route to Mexborough hardly features at all. That road was known as Back Lane a name that probably indicated its lack of importance.

Looking towards the centre of Swinton from the hump backed Hamshaw Bridge. Trams and other traffic then, as now, had to go up and over the hump back that carries the road over the Dearne & Dove Canal – then drive under the railway bridge of the North Midland Line. The photograph shows houses adjoining the Canal Tavern and small shops almost under the bridge – all long gone. One of the many coal trains is trundling over the road and pedestrians are taking a great interest in the photographer.

Station Street at the junction of Queen Street. The large building on the left was at one time used as an ex-servicemen's club. The first building on the right was Hammerton's shop which sold toys and other fancy goods. Possibly the little lad had his hoop bought from Mr Hammerton.

The Norman Arch. This was originally the chancel arch from Swinton's 12th century Norman chapel, which stood on the site of the present St. Margaret's Church hall. When the old chapel was demolished in the early years of the 19th Century, Mr Brameld, the pottery manufacturer saved this arch and the chapel's doorway. These were then reconstructed in the vicarage field near the north east corner of St. Margaret's Church. Sadly, the stone work did not stand up too well to being exposed to the elements and to atmospheric pollution. The arch was taken down for safety reasons in the 1940's.

[Left] Communion Cup from the old Norman chapel made in silver. The building had been deteriorating steadily prior to its demolition.
[Right] An item of silverware from the original Norman Chapel, it is dated 1765.

A very rare interior shot of the old church prior to its destruction by fire in 1897. The building was smaller than the present church with a shorter chancel. The high backed pews burnt like match wood once the fire took hold.

Exterior view of the old church. Only the tower survived the great fire of 1897. The tower still has evidence of fire damage visible on some of the interior timbers. That the tower was saved at all was as a result of the bravery of the firemen and was a very close run thing.

A fine external shot of St Michael's Church located on White Lee Road. After many years of procrastination the foundation stone for the church building was laid on 29th September 1900. St. Michael's was established to serve the growing population of Swinton Bridge and Roman Terrace, Mexborough. It closed in the 1960's and was later demolished.

Cliffield Road, Swinton with not a car in sight! The road ends in open fields and this shot was probably taken around the time of the First World War. The photographer was E.F. Turner of Swinton Post Office. The Turner family were sub-postmasters in Swinton for many years, Walter Turner taking the position in 1877. He was succeeded by his daughter when he retired.

A very busy scene at the bottom of Bridge Street near the road's junction with Market Street. Many small shops make up the former commercial area of 'Swinton Bridge' these also served as family homes for their proprietors. While many houses and commercial premises have been demolished, this range of buildings still remains as the offices of Brearley and Co. Accountants.

"Goose with two Necks,' *a very old inn located on Fitzwilliam Street close to the junction of Church Street. The remains of the pub doorway and window sills can still be made out on a wall near the present day McMahon Dance Studio. Fitzwilliam Street was formerly the main route through Swinton to the waterways at Kilnhurst. During the Georgian, period prior to the Victorian industrial boom, Fitzwilliam Street was the principal highway of the town and an axis for the built area.*

The Kings Head holds the oldest licence in the town dating from the 1700's. Originally a cottage conversion the building has been substantially altered over the years while retaining the original core. The dwelling at the side of the pub has gone and now forms the entrance to the car park. Arthur Hall was the Landlord at the time of this photograph, which was taken in the era of numerous telephone wires.

Fitzwilliam Street taken close to Manor Farm looking towards the direction of St. Margaret's Church. The little girl on the left in the white pinafore is standing where the Pinfold Estate begins. Only 2 properties remain today, Mirfield Cottage on the left and Orchard House on the right. Mirfield cottage is the oldest inhabited residence in Swinton and has records dating back to 1592.

This is an early shot of Milton Street, Swinton. The building with the flag pole is the original Travellers Rest which was little more than a large cottage. It was known that the notorious Sheffield based criminal and murderer Charles Peace used to frequent the Travellers and carried out various nefarious deals in there.

A view looking down Station Street towards the North Midland railway line. Most noteworthy is the large Congregational Church on the left, which later became the United Reformed Church. This particular building opened in August 1901 and could accommodate an amazing 500 worshippers, the last service held in the church was 8th May 2005.

A very fine shot of Station Street, Swinton in the 1920's. The three storied buildings on the left are the premises of Barnsley British Co-op. The road leading off to the left is Temperance Street while the greenery to the right is the land that would later be opened as the Harrop Gardens in 1932.

This small Chapel was the original Piccadilly Methodist Church built on land at the junction of Wentworth Road and Piccadilly Road. To the rear of the church can be seen open fields now the site of Harrop Drive and Glebe Road.

A stone laying ceremony at the Church Hall built on the site of Swinton's former Medieval Chapel in 1913. The block and tackle decorated with flowers for the occasion has been used to lower a foundation stone into place at the base of the main double doorway. Interesting to note are the original houses of Chapel Hill some of the residents can be seen looking out of their windows. These 3 storey dwellings were owned by the Wentworth Estate. Towards the end of their existence they were noted to be infested with cockroaches and other vermin. They were demolished in the early 1950's.

[Left] *"Stoneglen", 32 Church Street, taken in the 1920/1930's. The metal railings and gates were removed from most of Swinton's properties in the early 1940's as part of the war effort. Residents were not asked for permission. Men with cutting equipment and a lorry just came along and took the fine old metalwork!*

[Below] *The grand opening of the Carnegie Library on 25th June, 1905 by Sir William Holland MP., sited on the corner of Cliffield Road and Station Street the building was equipped with male and female reading rooms and a large lecture room for public meetings etc. A grant of £3,000 was secured from Andrew Carnegie to construct the building. This huge amount of money for the time would have equated in modern times to a major lottery grant being awarded to the town. It was largely thanks to the efforts of Fredrick Lee Harrop, at that time working as Solicitor and Town Clerk, that the funding was secured from the Carnegie Foundation. Andrew Carnegie was a Scottish born United States steel magnate, who had acquired incredible wealth as the U.S. economy grew. Carnegie was a great philanthropist with a personal commitment to improving access to free public libraries. Mexborough, Rawmarsh, Thorne, Tinsley and Walkley were some of the other South Yorkshire communities which benefited from Carnegie's generosity. It is hard to believe, given Mr. Carnegie's many responsibilities as head of a huge business empire and charitable foundation, that he took a personal interest in the progress of Swinton Library. It is, however, true as council records show, that he wanted the architect to change the plans and later Carnegie insisted that a clock be provided. It was the Scotsman's money so he had a perfect right to direct how it was spent giving his orders from far away U.S.A.! Carnegie was probably the greatest philanthropist of all time. He wrote a treatise on the virtues of giving away personal wealth, he certainly practiced what he preached. An extrapolation of the amounts he donated in his lifetime would indicate a figure in today's prices of about £22 billion!*

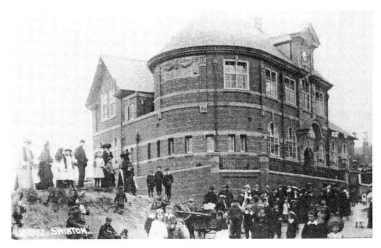

In 1920 "Highfields", Fitzwilliam Street, was made into Council Offices and one room became the chamber. The house was formerly occupied by Thomas and George Brameld of the Rockingham Pottery. The last private resident was Mr Frederick Lee Harrop, Solicitor and Clerk to the local board and Swinton Urban District Council from 1876 to 1919. Parts of the building were of great age as the original house dated from before the C16th. Highfields was demolished in the early 1980's and the site is now occupied by Highfield Court, Sheltered Housing Development.

To the rear of Highfield House were Swinton Urban District Council's pride and joy - these ornamental gardens and greenhouse. Children were soon seen off by the gardeners – this area was strictly out-of-bounds to unaccompanied youngsters. This view looks across to the direction of Swinton House Club. The Larches have been built between the Club and the site of the gardens.

A further view of the gardens to the rear of Highfield House. The building was an 'L' shaped former farm house stone gabled prior to becoming the private dwelling of Mr Harrop and subsequently the offices of Swinton Urban District Council.

Quite a well known photograph from around 1949/50. The structure at the entrance to Creighton Woods is known as the Sisters Lych Gate. Designed by Swinton Urban District Council's surveyor, Mr H Goodwin, the Lych Gate is built in oak and rustic brick. Miss Edith Harrop paid for the Lych Gate in tribute of the people of the Swinton District who served in the world wars. Miss Harrop wished the gate to be regarded as a joint gift from herself and her late sister Beatrice M R Harrop. The woods were purchased by the Council from the Earl Fitzwilliam for a nominal price in 1948. They were named Creighton Woods in honour of the Creighton Family which had given many years of public service to the Swinton area. Maurice Creighton was a County Alderman on the West Riding County Council.

Interior view of the Roxy Cinema which opened on 15th July 1929. Seat prices were:- pit, 4d; stalls 6d; and circle, 1 shilling. The Roxy was built by Wade & Son of Wath. The Cinema included an orchestra pit which can be seen in front of the screen. The Roxy provided entertainment for Swinton people till around late 1968 when it was closed. After closure the building stood empty for many years re-opening at one point as a short-lived skateboarding facility. It has since been Swinton Squash Club and at the time of writing is trading as Café Sport. The interior is unrecognisable from this photograph.

This photograph shows the exterior of the Roxy cinema taken around 1964. Also visible is the Globe self-service store, Swinton's fist supermarket type shop, a very small scale affair in comparison to today's mega-stores. Other shops in the parade are a pharmacy, Calladine & Son's (decorators), and Duke's ironmongers, the Robin Hood Pub sports a Magnet Ales sign. We would love to identify the lady in the white Macintosh and her little boy!

*An excellent shot of the original stone built Bow Broom Bridge which carried the road
that formed Queen Street over the North Midland Railway line and the Dearne &
Dove Canal. Many people are enjoying angling by the canal or just sitting along the
towpath in the sunshine. The railway lines are just out of shot to the right.*

*A display cabinet, made from oak by a
Mexborough based craftsman, Tony Jones,
provided to Swinton library for the display of a
range of pottery produced in the town. Funding
for the cabinet and purchase of most of the pottery
collection was raised by voluntary effort
organised by Swinton Heritage.*

Travellers Rest 1930s building which replaced the smaller earlier public house. Stone cottages stand right up to the pub wall in an area which now forms the car park.

A fine shot of the rear of Swinton House taken whilst it was still a private residence. The tennis court can be seen between the building and the tree line. This building dates from the C18th, it is built of coursed grey stone, patched with cement. An arched pedimented doorway allowed access from the front centre, this has been blocked up for many years.

Wardle's Farm stood at the junction of Church Street and Golden Smithies Lane on land that now forms the Gate Pub's car park. This photograph dates from the Second World War period. The "S" sign on the trolley wire pole indicates the direction of the nearest air raid shelter.

Newly built Council properties on Rig Drive. The estate was named Wood Farm after the Farm which is was built upon. In this photograph, some of the properties have yet to be allocated to the first lucky tenants.

A birds-eye view of the Beeches, its' gardens and out buildings. This property was just off Fitzwilliam Street where the cul-de-sac of the same name now stands. The Beeches was a three-storied house built in the 19th century of local coursed stone. As can be seen in this photograph, it had a projecting porch and a central palladian window on the first floor.

Aged persons bungalows on Chapel Hill just after construction in 1956 before the roadway has been surfaced. Notice the lack of any TV aerials and garden paths have yet to be constructed. Some three storey houses stood on this site prior to the laying out of the St John's estate.

This early 1960's shot shows the original Butchers Arms pub at the junction of Station Street and Queen Street. All the buildings on the left were swept away when Swinton Shopping precinct and Harrop Garden Flats were constructed in the early 1970's.

Not long before demolition, this picture shows the Old Butchers Arms and parade of shops on Station Street. The two cyclists are just passing a branch of 'Barker the Baker'.

The Ebenezer Church stood on Milton Street from 1873 till it was demolished in 2000. New residential flats have been built on the site and the developer kindly agreed to retain the original church name plate in the boundary wall. This photograph shows the plaque being re-laid by the authors of this book while former church members look on.

Drawing by Swinton Fitzwilliam Junior School pupil Daniel Camplin, which was featured as the cover of a highly popular "Swinton Then and Now" calendar produced in 2003. Daniel's drawing was selected by a panel of local people – he won prizes for himself and his school.

Swinton Town Cross or Butter Cross or Market Cross originally stood near to the old Norman Chapel which occupied the site of St. Margaret's Church Hall. The structure would have acted as a meeting point and a place to trade. People would have given their word in front of the cross and this was not something that would have been done lightly. The cross was an early symbol of Christianity in the district and along with the Chapel, would have been viewed with affection by the local people. Both the Chapel and cross stood on land originally owned by the famous Knights of St. John of Jerusalem. During the period of religious iconoclasm (destruction of religious signs and images) of the 16th and 17th centuries, Swinton's Cross along with many others throughout the Country were destroyed. We cannot be certain as to how the original cross would have looked; this is lost in the mists of time. It could possibly have been made of wood or stone. The shape may have been as the restored octagonal style, capped with a Saltaire or Maltese cross. A Celtic cross would have been unlikely. A small plain cross surmounting a fairly narrow shaft is a further possibility. All that was left was a sandstone plinth and a magnesium limestone base as seen in this photograph. When the old Norman Chapel was pulled down at the beginning of the C19th the cross base was removed to the vicarage field of the new St. Margaret's Church. The cross remains were once again shifted to stand just south of the church's west doorway about 1 metre from the tower as seen in this shot. It remained here until 2004 when a project was carried out to preserve the old stonework, restore the cross to its former glory and return it to its original location.

*The remains of the Chancel Arch of Swinton's former Norman Chapel in a state of
ruination in the grounds of the Vicarage field. This photograph, taken prior to
consolidation work funded from the National lottery shows how unsafe the arch had
become and close to total destruction.*

The topography of Swinton inevitably means that some locations can be prone to flooding in severe weather. This shot is taken at the bottom of Temperance Street where it joins Manor Road. At this point, people who lived in this part of town used to draw their water supply from a stream named the Brookfield Ditch. The ditch is now culveted and runs beneath the road (except when floods like this occur!) The rather dilapidated white building on the left of the road has now gone and the flats of Horsefair Close occupy this site. Older houses built on this area were formerly referred to as 'The Dogem' - though we don't know why.

More flooding on the low lying open space between Cliff Bank and Brookfield Avenue. A younger resident tries a session of underwater cycling!

A torrent of water flows down behind garages at the bottom of Cliffield Road. The flow follows the course of the Brookfield Ditch which drains into the Sheffield and South Yorkshire Navigation.

These two young people are sat in the top north east corner of the land adjacent to Swinton churchyard. To the left of the youngsters can be seen part of the remains of The Roman Ridge Dyke which passes along the boundary of the church land and the open fields beyond. The earthwork known as the Roman Ridge runs across South-West Yorkshire from Wincobank in Sheffield to Hilltop in Kimberworth. There it splits into two, one dyke goes to Swinton Common and Kilnhurst while the second branch (pictured) runs to Mexborough. The Dyke is very old and nobody knows who built it, when or why. The green field beyond the dyke has a modern housing development built upon it now known as Far Golden Smithies.

TRANSPORT

This view shows Swinton's first railway station built on the North Midland line in 1840. In 1899 a new station was built towards the north of the Station Street Bridge. This 2nd Station served the town until its closure in 1968. In 1990 Swinton's present day interchange opened on the original site of the 1840 building.

During the construction of the Mexborough and Swinton Tramway in 1907 extensive and disruptive roadway excavation was required as this photograph taken in Mexborough High Street illustrates. Not only were rails required but miles of copper cabling to carry the underground power supply. Huge cable drums can be seen in this shot and the entire road appears to be closed off, no doubt to the great annoyance of the local shop proprietors.

*At last came the great day when the route was opened to passengers on 3ʳᵈ August,
1907. As can be seen in this photograph, people flocked to ride on and see the new
route. In the first 3 days an astonishing 40,000 people were carried bringing in revenue
to the company of £300. Nine cars were used initially and these soon proved to be sadly
inadequate for the volume of passenger numbers. The first building on the left stands at
the junction of White Lee Road and Bridge Street, it was at one time a pub known as
'The Crown'. On the right the first building is the 'Red House' pub.*

*Bridge Street on the opening day of the new tramway in 1907. The 'Dolter' studs
which supplied the power to the cars can be seen very well, spaced about 9 feet apart.
The single line and passing places are visible. Local residents and shopkeepers have
turned out to observe this historic occasion.*

We can date this view of Bridge Street fairly accurately to 1907/08 due to the lack of overhead wires. Power was supplied by means of contact studs on the ground between the rails. Also the tram car is of the open top double-decker style, which was the first type of car employed.

An accident on old Warren Vale Road on 30th July, 1908, fortunately no one was seriously injured. The car was No. 14 which had been operating the 5.00 am Rotherham to Mexborough service. Car 14 ran out of control down the 1 in 9 Warren Vale Hill and ended up on its side. 30th July, 1908 was quite a memorable day as the overhead wires were completed from Rotherham to the Swinton boundary.

Looking down Church Street, the photographer is stood at the side of St Margaret's Church Hall as a tram approaches. This shot shows how narrow the road was at this location with what was a row of properties known as Milton Cottages sticking well out on the right of the picture. In 1930 the highway was widened and some of the buildings on the right were demolished to improve the sight lines of the bend. The left hand side of the road has not changed at all with regards to St John's Church and the houses.

This image taken from Bridge Street looking back to Hamshaw Bridge shows the considerable gradient that the tram cars were required to negotiate. Of the properties on the left nothing remains, the site is now occupied by a petrol station.

Out in Warren Vale countryside the crew of car 13 strike a post for the camera while waiting the arrival of another car at this passing place. Note the good view of the studs between the rails. This shot was taken shortly after the opening.

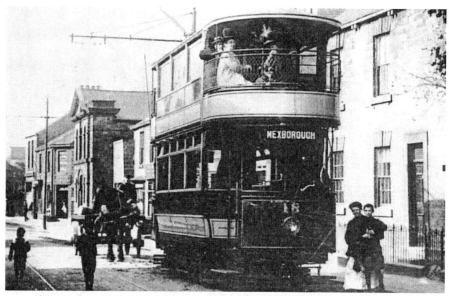

Station Street, Swinton just past the junction of Queen Street around 1910. Mexborough and Swinton tram no.18 pauses on its journey to Mexborough. The tramway consisted of double lines at this point but was single line in other locations. Close examination of the shops beyond the rear tram-wire support pole reveals a striped barber's pole – these premises still house a gent's hairdressers (2005).

Car 13 again but by 1908 a low covered top was provided, we think that it is the same platform crew as in the earlier shot opposite!

During the First World War to fill the gaps in the workforce left by men joining the fighting forces many previously male dominated jobs were opened-up for women. A female bus conductress working on car 19 provides a classic example of how women were able to step into the jobs left by men called to war.

This photograph shows Old Warren Vale Road in the bottom with New Warren Vale Road on the higher ground, taken during construction of the new road in 1930. Old Warren Vale Road was (and still is) very narrow and even with the light motor traffic of the time the route was proving inadequate. The construction of the new road provided much needed work as many men in the area were unemployed due to the recession that began with the Wall Street Crash. A deep cutting was created and a concrete bridge built to carry the new road over the Collier Brook.

A shot taken from Bow Broom Bridge looking towards the Manvers colliery and coking work complex. The Dearne and Dove Canal dominates the centre of photograph with the North Midland Railway's lines to the right. In the distance can be made out Wath Road Junction Signal Box and the Branch to Bolton-upon-Dearne known as the Swinton and Knottingley Railway (S&K).

Close to the junction of the Sheffield & South Yorkshire Navigation a small craft is moored near some very old buildings aside the Dearne & Dove Canal. The largest of these buildings once served as a boatman's mission for the use of barge families and horse marines, who hired out their horses to pull the barges along. The long dark building looming in the background is one of the larger structures of the G.E.C complex.

A 1960's view looking down Church Street at the junction of Golden Smithies Lane and Highfield Road. On the left of the picture just in front of the first shop there used to stand a toll house for the collection of tolls from road users. The area still retains the name of Toll Bar and 'The Gate' pub has its origins from the Highway Turnpike era. Traffic seems very light in comparison to today.

A Mexborough and Swinton Traction Company trolley-bus climbs towards the Hamshaw hump back bridge on Bridge Street. The first trolley bus passed through Swinton in 1928, they were so successful that the trams were with drawn a year after. This model was known as a Sunbeam, the centre doors are noteworthy. All services had a conductor to collect the fares.

Trolley bus 33 emerges from the dive-under of the Midland railway bridge. A number of low bridges were to be found along the various routes of the Mexborough and Swinton the service therefore was obliged to employ single deck trolley buses to allow the wires to remain clear of the vehicles roof.

This photograph shows a Rotherham bound M & S trolley bus passing the company's main depot at Dale Road, Rawmarsh, which was later taken over by Yorkshire Traction.

A smaller depot was located at Toll Bar in Mexborough. This building still exists and is currently used by a tyre company.

Heading out of Mexborough a trolley bus is about to pass beneath the first of two railway bridges. It is interesting to observe the way that the power lines were off-set towards the centre of the road. The trolley poles on top of the vehicle were quite flexible, and supported by strong springs.

Mexborough and Swinton Fleet No. 22 on the number 8 service – Rotherham to Mexborough. Here the vehicle passes the junction of Romwood Avenue as it descends Rockingham Road. The most remarkable difference between this image and today is the very narrowness of the road at this point. The situation was resolved with the demolition of the stone houses on the right of the picture. Newer houses were built further back from the road and widening was carried out on both sides. Rockingham Road was formerly known as Pottery Lane. During the construction of a cellar in 1853 a hoard of roman coins was uncovered. The coins had examples of all the Roman Emperors from 69 to 212 AD, who left them – we shall never know.

Mexborough and Swinton Number 8 trolley bus seen here emerging on the Swinton side of the twin railway over-bridges on Rowms Lane. To the rear of the vehicle the advertising placard promotes Bristol tipped cigarettes at just 3s 6d for 20 (about 17.5p). The placard is still on site but prices have risen considerably.

Very close to the end of trolley-bus operation, this rather poignant shot shows the shape of things to come. A Mexborough & Swinton trolley-bus turns to cross the Sheffield & South Yorkshire canal next to the Mexborough Toll Bar Depot, while close on it's tail, is a diesel bus in the company's green and cream livery.

The last day of Trolley Bus operation through Swinton was on 26th March, 1961. This ended 45 years of service in which they had run a total of 39 million miles and carried 382 million passengers. This photograph shows the specially decorated lead vehicle of a final convoy ascending Rockingham Road, residents stand at their doors to bid their farewell to this popular, quiet, environmentally friendly form of transport.

A Yorkshire Traction single-decker negotiates the Woodman round-a-bout in this mid 1960's photograph. The shop and house in the centre of the picture were owned by the Parkes family for many years. Redundant trolley wire poles are still in evidence awaiting removal. Trolley bus services finished in 1961.

90265 was the last locomotive to leave Mexborough Motive Power Depot (located on Swinton Meadows) on 1ˢᵗ May, 1964. Railwaymen posing to commemorate the occasion were: top left to right: D. Smith (Labourer); R. Sidebottom (Telephone Attendant); W. Smith (Fireman); D. Trash (Fireman); bottom left to right: G. Hobson (Driver); D. Tongue (Foreman); R. F. Hague (Driver); G. Guy (Fireman); G. Lindley (Fireman), A. Eyre (Fireman); M. Cooper (Foreman Cleaner); J. Tingle (Fire-dropper); G. Spencer (Driver) ?? E. Foster (Tool-man); W. Skinns (Shunter).

Swinton Junction Signal Box was located on the North Midland Line just North of the 1899 Swinton Town Station. The box controlled the junction which allowed trains to cross to the Great Central lines via the Swinton Curve. Points also connected the railway sidings within Swinton Glass Works. The box was taken out in 1973 and nothing remains today to show it ever existed.

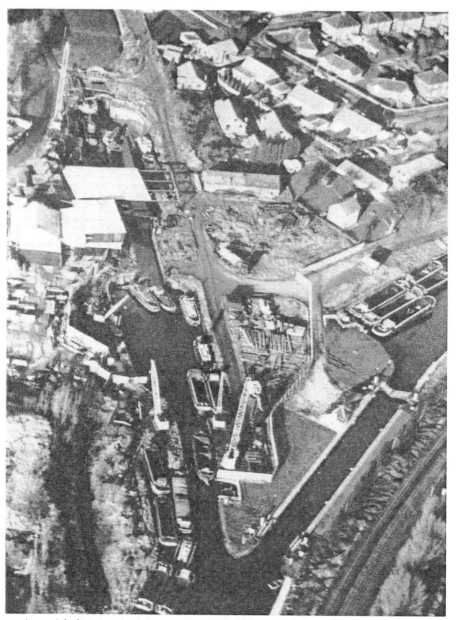

An aerial photograph of the junction of the Dearne and Dove, Sheffield and South Yorkshire Navigations at Swinton. Waddington's boat building premises can be seen along with their heavy duty cranes. Many barges crowd both waterways and the long Swinton Lock has it's Western gates opened.

This is a view of the former Coach House of Swinton House built in the 18ᵗʰ Century. Swinton House was once the residence of the Otter family, Mr. Otter was the local magistrate. The cellars of the property were sometimes used as cells to hold prisoners on a temporary basis prior to their removal to local courts for trial.

Adwick Crossing was located on the Great Central/LNER line from Wath to Mexborough, where Golden Smithies Lane crossed the railway. Various pit top buildings of the Manvers Colliery complex can be seen. The signal box which controlled the crossing stood to the right of the gates.

Artist's impression of how the Dearne and Dove canal spur could look if sufficient funding could be acquired to improve the towpaths.

A further view shows the 'Ship' side of Hamshaw Bridge. At the time of writing the seats are in position, the dam is built and some surfacing has been installed. The landscape, however, still leaves much to be desired.

WORK

C.T Butterfield is one of the regions oldest established family funeral directors. The company first started trading in Swinton in 1874 when John Butterfield (pictured), a master wheelwright, moved into the town. For the full story of the Butterfield company see "A Yorkshire Undertaking" by Ken Wyatt ISBN 1-904706-04-5.

*An early shot. Interior of Hattersley Brothers, Queens' Foundry Production line.
Visible are a range of components of Hattersley's products and some very young
looking apprentices.*

*A very early group of workers at Hattersley Brothers, Queens Foundry. The plant
eventually covered some 10 acres and became very prosperous and successful
enterprise. The youth of some of the workers is noteworthy. Young lads came to work
direct from School to learn the trades of the iron foundry industry. Many of them
would stay with the Company till retirement.*

This view is taken inside the pattern making shop. Over the years products from the factory were exhibited at such show case events as the British Industries Fair, Ideal Home Exhibition and elsewhere. The site was used for a period by Mr C H Verity for the manufacture of Railway Wheels and Wagons.

This shot is taken inside the Council Chamber of the former Swinton U.D.C. office at Highfield House. The original offices of S.U.D.C. were situated in the building that now serves as the Masonic Hall on Station Street.

Many workplaces developed a tradition of annual works outings. Ward and Sons obligingly provided transport in the shape of one of the firm's motor lorries for the workers outing in about 1930. This photograph gives us many fine details of the Ward and Sons premises in Market Street. In among the advertising paintwork is the proud statement that the company were bottlers of Bass Ales.

Queen Foundry's works outing was no exception and this smiling group are about to board the coach to go on a fishing trip in the 1950s.

The LNER sports and social club on Rowms Lane on the occasion of the opening of the club. The event was attended by Senior Managers of the British Railways Board North Eastern Division and Officers of the British Railways Staff Association. Many of the members were railway workers at the nearby Mexborough Locomotive Depot and yards. The original building was breeze blocks and corrugated sheeting.

The club is formally opened and the key is symbolically handed over by Mr. K.L. Bird General Manager of the North Eastern Region of British Railways. The key is received by Mr. Pursehouse the Club Secretary while Mr. George Hobson the Club Chairman looks on (Mr. Hobson was a loco driver at Mexborough depot).

A view taken inside the wages office of Baker and Bessemer Works. The earliest reference to metal industry on the site of the Baker and Bessemer Works was in 1828 but earlier activity is most likely. Various ups and downs and changes of ownership occurred up to 1903 when John Baker purchased the enterprise from John Brown & Co. of Sheffield. After Baker's death his sons continued to build up the business. In 1929 John Baker & Co. purchased some 90% of the shares of the Henry Bessemer & Co. Ltd., and the name of the company changed to John Baker & Bessemer Ltd. During both World Wars, production of war materials was carried out at a frantic pace 24 hours a day. Eventually, the site of the Kilnhurst Steel Works covered around 30 acres.

Teenager Tony Capstick receiving training in his first job as a 'Train Register Lad' in a Mexborough Signal Box (which we believe to be Mexborough No.3). The clock says 11.30, so Tony has probably been on duty since 06:00. He looked very smartly turned out in his clean white shirt with his sleeves rolled up for work.

Inside the men's reading room of the old Carnegie Library. The sexes were kept separate to avoid any hanky-panky. Libraries were places where people went to study, not to flirt!

Clifton House School, Crossland Street, Swinton. This was a small private school later becoming a dwelling house. It is now converted into flats.

The business premises of T Cross, 106 Bridge Street, just one of the many shops that could be found in this part of town. Signs on the shop advise would be customers that it is a family grocer and dealer in wines, spirits, beers and stouts. A lad with a barrow stands near the entrance waiting for deliveries.

This rather damaged photograph shows Rawden's Boot & Shoe shop which was located on Queen Street. One of Mr Rawden's staple trades was making and repairing pit boots for the area's many coal miners.

Swinton branch of the Barnsley British Co-operative Society Grocery Department, located on Station Street. Three staff, in spotlessly clean shirts and aprons, pose for the camera, one of their children has also got in on the act! The windows display a very neat, artistic display of tinned and dry goods. An attempt was made to form a Swinton Co-operative Society, in 1864, 41 members were enrolled. The venture failed unlike the Kilnhurst Co-op which was a great success. The mighty Barnsley British provided co-operative retail services for the town from the last decades of the 19th century.

A further row of Co-op retail premises on Station Street. Swinton was known as the 21st Branch of the Barnsley British society. These premises included drapery department, woollens, footwear, a tailor, gent's outfitters and a lending library where books could be borrowed for a modest fee.

Station Street close to the junction of Queen Street was in competition with Bridge Street as a commercial area. By comparison with today's traffic congestion the main thoroughfare looks remarkably peaceful in this earlier view. The small white dog would have a very short life span if it were to wander in the roadway at this location today.

Gate Inn prior to extensions being made. The women folk stand at the pub doorway while the sign above the door advises that John Hague holds the licence. He was permitted to retail wines, spirits, beer, tobacco and all kinds of produce bought and sold on commission. The pub took its name form a nearby toll gate on the highway.

The Toll Bar commercial area on Church Street taken in the 1950's. Shops on view are H.E. Hughes, Toll Bar Fruit Stores and Swinton Common Post Office, which closed down in 2004. Little has changed other than the names of businesses operating from the shop units. The small older buildings at the side of the van have mainly gone to be replaced by 'The Cabin' shop.

Completed in the late 1940's the Highfield Farm Estate included 8 shop units located on Broadway to service the local market. The shops have flats above and have changed hands many times over the years.

A very old photograph of the head gear of Swinton Common Colliery. The pit top and shaft were located on the open land between Woodlands Crescent and Creighton Woods. A small obelisk marks the location of the shaft – the pit closed in the early 1920's.

This photograph shows the demolition of the pit top buildings of Swinton Common Colliery. In the background can be seen the woodlands that were to become Creighton Woods. First planted in the late C18th the woods are mainly beeches and oaks, evidence of coal mining activity scars parts of the woodlands.

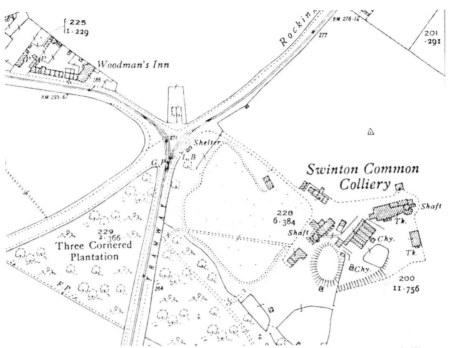

This map shows the extent of the buildings which served Swinton Common Colliery. The cross roads in the centre of the map are the site of the Woodman round-a-bout. No doubt the "Woodman's Inn" was well positioned to quench the thirsts of the miners at the end of their shift.

A photograph of the original Woodman's Inn on Warren Vale Road. The building to the immediate rear of the pub was once a butcher's shop; it is now incorporated in the pub's 'tap room'. The row of terraced houses, at the side of the road continuing towards Wath, are long gone.

Tyas Guest Memorial Masons' yard, this was located opposite the entrance to St. Margaret's Church just below the Ring O' Bells pub. This company were real masters of their trade  *and many fine examples of the memorial masons' art can be seen in St. Margaret's churchyard and other local burial grounds.*

 *This aerial photograph of the Swinton Works of the General Electric Company (G.E.C.) shows the extent of the plant located at Swinton Meadows between the Sheffield and South Yorkshire Navigation and the River Don. The factory was a former munitions factory making armour piercing bombs and aircraft components. At the end of the war the works were acquired by the Birmingham Cooker works of the* G.E.C. Unprecedented demands for electric cookers during the post-war period both in the U.K. and the export market ensured that this site became the biggest cooker factory in the British Empire. The first cooker was assembled and dispatched on 27th June 1946, only a remarkable 3 months after the factory was acquired by the G.E.C. Today the site is owned and operated by Morphy Richards for warehousing, packaging and distribution. A customer call and contact centre is also located within the site and some 300 people are employed.*

Dale Brown & Co.'s crane unloads sand for the glass works from a barge on the Dearne & Dove Canal. While the last through journey from Swinton to Barnsley took place before World War 2, coal was loaded out of Manvers by barge into the 1950's. An occasional load of sand was delivered by barge to the glass works until the early 1970's.

Dale Brown and Co Glass Works, White Lee Road, in the early 1960's. Glassmaking has been established as an industry in Swinton since the 1850's. Dale Browns took over these premises in 1913 and invested in modern automated machinery. A wide range of glass containers were produced on site with production exceeding 1 million units weekly in the 1950's. The crane in the centre of the picture was used to unload sand from barges on the spur of the Dearne & Dove Canal. Swinton Glass works went on to change hands a number of times finally ending in the ownership of United Glass Containers, part of the Guinness Group. Despite full order books, a highly skilled workforce and modern glass making equipment, the glassworks were closed in 1988 resulting in job losses to over 400 employees.

A fine study of the Dearne and Dove canal locks and the Ship Inn. The 3 chimneys dominating the skyline are the Dale-Browns Glassworks.

Farmer Mr. Mawson ploughing with a pair of horses in fields next to Creighton woods.

Farmer Mr Lines gathers together his ducks in his yard to the rear of Hawthorne Farm on Fitzwilliam Street. Mr Lines was the milk rounds-man to many Swinton properties.

Poster announcing the opening programmes at the new Swinton Picture House which opened its' doors on 15th July 1925.

An advertising flyer for the builders Trowbridge & Trowbridge. Frederick Trowbridge started the building business which at the time of this document was being operated by Edward George (Eddie) Trowbridge and John Frederick (Jack) Trowbridge. Eddie kept the books and managed the business.

TROWBRIDGE
&
TROWBRIDGE

BUILDERS and
CONTRACTORS

SWINTON

TELEPHONE   MEXBOROUGH 2196

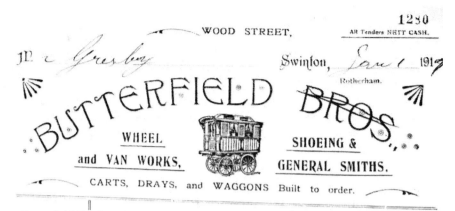

Butterfield Brothers letterhead demonstrates the various services. supplied by the business. John Butterfield who began the company in 1874 was a master wheelwright, vans and wagons were built at the Wood Street premises. Gypsy caravans and show-mans' vans were a speciality. The building that was the Smithy is now the Chapel of Rest at the current funeral directors premises.

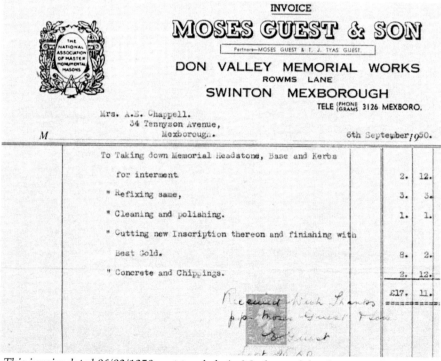

This invoice dated 06/09/1950 sent to a lady in Mexborough has been sent from Moses Guest and Son of Rowms Lane. Partners at this time were Moses, Guest and T.J. Tyas Guest, the area of the Don Valley Memorial Works is today occupied as storage area for A.M.B. Products. Mrs. Chappell made prompt payment which was received with thanks on 20th September, 1950.

This building was a former village butchers shop located next to Hawthorne Farm on Fitzwilliam Street. It was demolished to facilitate the development of Hawthorne Chase which now occupies the site.

Standing just off Market Street these buildings were once part of Ward & Sons Mineral Water and bottling works. In 1874 William Ward founder of the company established a Mineral Water works in Market Street. About 1900 Ward & Sons commenced to bottle ale from the famous Bass and Worthington companies. As the company grew throughout the first half of the C20[th] the most up to date bottling, corking, labelling and filtering machinery was acquired. In the 1950's, the company could report the capacity to turn out 7,000 bottles per hour. The site expanded to cover 2 acres, employed 120 people and operated a large fleet of delivery lorries. The plant closed, however, and in later years the works were occupied by Jackson's Building Centre. Jackson's in turn have invested in purpose built premises to the front of the old Ward's site as their business has outgrown the old bottling works, during 2005 these buildings have been demolished.

Swinton Stables and Farm, Golden Smithies Lane, not long before these buildings were tragically demolished. The stables complex was established to train the race horses of the Earl Fitzwilliam and were well served by the Swinton Racecourse training ground just to the rear. Through the years the training facilities were used by other trainers including Mr Smallwood and Bob McCormack. A number of notable winners trained in Swinton including the 'Lincoln' Winner Squadron Castle. An early school room was created in one of the stables haylofts with Mr Willoughby Wood as the villages' first school master. These primitive educational arrangements continued until the opening of Fitzwilliam Junior School in 1853.

Former kiln of the Swinton Don Pottery, not long before demolition stands forlornly in Don Pottery Yard just off Rowms Lane. At one time the kiln was used as a home by a local man with alcohol problems known as 'Dusty Herbert'. The Don Pottery was established in about 1800 when John Green obtained a plot of swampy ground close to the Sheffield and South Yorkshire Navigation. The site had the advantage of having a wharf, which was ideal for transporting the fragile finished pottery goods away by barge. Along with the aid of his partners, John Green developed one of Yorkshires finest potteries, the products of which are highly collectable in the antiques world.

A fire at the Nut & Bolt premises on White Lee Road in 2004

A South Yorkshire Fire Service tender pumps water for the fire fighters dealing with the blaze

Queens Foundry main office block taken while in the ownership of Stelrad and before the company car park was surfaced.

At the end of the year long Miners strike 1984-85, Mineworkers from Kilnhurst pit, their families and supporters march back to work together behind their Union banner. Here the procession moves in a proud and dignified manner along Lime Grove.

Wharin's shop on Cliffield Road displays a very impressive range of fresh meat in the window.

10th November, 1998, saw TV personality, Ian Clayton, in Swinton with a film crew recording a feature on the Rockingham Pottery Waterloo Kiln. At the same time, Ian was 'ambushed' into performing the unveiling of a cabinet displaying locally manufactured pottery in Swinton Library. This event was also incorporated in the television broadcast.

A (mainly) smiling class photograph taken at Swinton Fitzwilliam Junior School around 1990. The teacher is Mr. Baker girl pupils include Clair Pendlebury, Zoe Lant and Amy Brearley. Boys include David Appleyard, Jonathan Pendlebury (who went on to become a professional rugby player) and Robert Coward (who went on to achieve success in the boxing ring).

Swinton's Member of Parliament, John Healey, a treasury minister, conducts the official opening of the newly re-furbished offices of Brearley & Co on Bridge Street. John is being greeted by Giles Brearley in this shot, taken in 2002. Swinton is in the Wentworth Parliamentary Constituency, and John became MP for the area in 1997, following the retirement of Peter Hardy.

An episode of the BBC TV comedy "I didn't know you cared" was filmed in Swinton in the late 1970's. Here, cast members and the film crew can be seen on Dun Street. An interested crowd of local people look on from Hamshaw Bridge. The filming involved temporary road closures.

In this shot, the cast can be seen outside the Red House Pub, which was re-named "The Bargeman's Comfort" for the filming. The sitcom ran for 4 series, with 27 episodes transmitted between 1975-79. It was based on novels by Peter Tinniswood.

Characters included the wonderfully miserable Uncle Mort and the Brandon family. Les Brandon spent most of his time trying to avoid the sharp tongue of his wife Annie. Carter Brandon was an easy going type who wanted to get through life with as little fuss and bother as possible. His wife Pat, however had other ideas, she wanted her husband to become a "young executive". Uncle Stanley wondered around with a cardboard box containing the ashes of his best mate – his catchphrase was "I heard that- pardon?".